POP CULTURE BIOS
ACTION MOVIE STARS

JENNIFER LAWRENCE

THE HUNGER GAMES' GIRL ON FIRE

NADIA HIGGINS

Lerner Publications Company
MINNEAPOLIS

Lerner Publications Company
A division of Lerner Publishing Group, Inc.
241 First Avenue North
Minneapolis, MN 55401 U.S.A.

Website address: www.lernerbooks.com

Library of Congress Cataloging-in-Publication Data

Higgins, Nadia.
    Jennifer Lawrence : The hunger games' girl on fire / by
Nadia Higgins.
       p.   cm. — (Pop culture bios: action movie stars)
    Includes index.
    ISBN 978-1-4677-0743-5 (lib. bdg. : alk. paper)
    ISBN 978-1-4677-1012-1 (eBook)
    1. Lawrence, Jennifer, 1990—Juvenile literature. 2. Actors—
United States—Biography—Juvenile literature. I. Title.
PN2287.L28948H55 2013
791.4502'8092—dc23 [B]   2012031010

Manufactured in the United States of America
2 – BP – 6/1/13

It's March 2012, and *The Hunger Games* is about to hit theaters everywhere. That means Jennifer Lawrence's life is about to change big time. Is she ready? *Late Show* host David Letterman wants to know.

"I've been shaking for, like, two months straight," she says, smiling. She's kidding. *We think.*

As any Jen fan knows, she plays the starring role in the *Games*. She's Katniss. And early reviews said that she was amazing. They said she nailed the biggest female role since Bella in *Twilight*.

Jen donned this sophisticated dress when she appeared on *The Late Show* in March 2012.

So what would Jen be worried about? "I'm a troll. I hate myself. I think the movie was great, but their biggest mistake was me," she spills, only part jokingly, to Letterman. Letterman looks at her like she's nuts. He pretends to write notes on a pad like a therapist. That cracks Jen up.

Jen can't help but worry about the tidal wave of pressure that's about to crash on her. Screaming fans make her feel weird, she says. And those red carpet events are so scary. She's fessed up that she's already tripped

Jen signs autographs for fans after appearing on *The Late Show*.

PREMIERE =
an early showing of a
movie for reviewers and
other media people

"massively" at two *Hunger Games* premieres. It's something anybody could have done. But it freaks Jen out when the whole world sees her every stumble!

There's another problem too. Jen gets hyper when she's nervous. "Then I go in interviews and say things like, 'I'm like a Chihuahua. I'm shaking and peeing!'" Jen laughs. "Then afterwards I'm like, 'I just talked about peeing on the red carpet!'"

By now, the whole *Late Show* crowd is rolling in the aisles. Jen can't stop laughing either. Letterman really can't wait to see the movie now, he says. "I got to have more of this!" he exclaims. He's so right. Watching Jennifer entertain—or even just have a friendly chat—really is a treat!

Jen glammed up for a *Hunger Games* premiere in March 2012.

Jen and her dad, Gary, in September 2012

CHAPTER ONE

KENTUCKY GIRL

FROM LEFT: Jen sits next to her mother, Karen; her publicist, Liz Mahoney; and actress Casey MacLaren at a film festival brunch in January 2010.

Fans have tons of reasons for loving Jennifer Lawrence. She's funny. She's fierce. She's beautiful. But of all of Jen's superpowers, one stands out the most. You can't look at her face without wondering what she's thinking.

That's because Jen is, first of all, an actor. A total natural. An Oscar-nominated artist who's never even taken an acting class. Jen says this job never felt like a choice. She *had* to do it. But it took her a little while to find that out.

NOMINATED =
picked to be part of a group of people who have a chance at winning an award

Wild Child

Jennifer Shrader Lawrence was born on August 15, 1990, in Louisville, Kentucky. She grew up outside the city on a horse farm. Her mom, Karen, ran a summer camp at the farm. Her dad, Gary, headed up a construction business. Jen has two older brothers, Blaine and Ben.

Jennifer remembers her childhood as "so lovely." But she has to laugh while she says that because she did so much crazy stuff. For example, she spent a lot of time riding horses. But the horses weren't broken in yet. *And* she didn't use a saddle. Jen got kicked and thrown more times than she can remember.

Jen grew up in this house near Louisville, Kentucky.

Jen's brothers kept her on her toes too. The way she tells it, the three kids fought—a lot. After every fight, their mom made them say "the eleven words...*I love you. I'm sorry. Please forgive me. I was wrong.*" Today, Jen and her brothers are super tight.

As a kid, Jen spent lots of time outside. Besides riding horses, she fished. She made slingshots and played war in the backyard.

THAT'S SO MEAN!

One time Jen's brothers pinned her legs behind her head. Then they smeared peanut butter over her face. *Then* they got their three dogs to come lick it off! Nice, right?

Jen played softball and field hockey. She was on the boys' basketball team too. In middle school, she got into cheerleading. Jen had so much energy that she had trouble sitting still!

While Jen loved her cocurricular activities, she didn't love being in the classroom. She *had* to sit still when her teacher was talking! She got antsy. And she remembers feeling dumber than the other kids (even though she pretty much always got As and Bs). Plus, seeing kids bully others, and sometimes being bullied herself, really bummed her out. School just wasn't Jen's thing.

Jen (TOP LEFT) cheered for her school during seventh grade.

Jen considers herself a "good girl." As a teen, she never drank or sneaked out of the house. The worst thing on Jen's rap sheet? Sticking gum under the table.

Jen was about to find out exactly what her "thing" was. As it turned out, it was acting. Jen had been in church and school plays since she was nine. She'd had fun but wasn't hooked—yet. Then, when she was fourteen, Jen had a magical moment. She read a script for something she was thinking of trying out for. "I just fell in love," she dished to *Glamour* magazine. For the first time in her life, she felt like she understood something 100 percent. "I didn't feel stupid anymore," Jen recalled.

She <3s New York

Jen was sure, more than sure. She wanted to be an actor. She convinced her mom to take her to New York City for spring break. Jen's plan was to spend her vacation applying at talent agencies.

Jen's eighth-grade school picture

One day, Jen and her mom were watching break-dancers perform outside. A man with a camera came up to them. He asked to take Jen's picture. The random guy was a modeling scout. And that random meeting would lead to Jen landing an agent!

AGENT =
a person whose job it is to help actors get jobs

The agent wanted Jen to come back that summer and give acting a shot. There was just one problem. Jen's parents didn't want her to drop out of school and move to New York at the age of fourteen. (Imagine that!) Still, Jen spent months begging them. Finally, they agreed to a trial period. Jen could go to the city for six weeks that summer. Her brother Blaine, who was nineteen, would go with her.

Jen's parents thought she would get acting out of her system. Instead, she got calls for auditions. Then she got booked. Her first job was a part in an MTV commercial. Then came small parts in the TV series *Monk* and *Cold Case*. Jen's dream was coming true!

AUDITION =
a tryout for an acting job

Jen at the premiere of *The Burning Plain* in 2008

CHAPTER TWO

MAKIN' IT

Jen (CENTER) poses with Bill Engvall (FAR LEFT) and other fellow *Bill Engvall Show* cast members in 2007.

In 2005, Jen's mother moved to New York to be with her. But things weren't easy. Jen didn't have any friends in her new home. Plus, she still had to finish high school. Her parents weren't giving in on that point. Jen put in long hours alone in her room studying. But she did it. In fact, she got her degree two years early.

Meanwhile, the acting ball kept on rolling. Soon, Jennifer and her mom moved to Los Angeles. Jen had decided that she wanted to be a part of that city's hopping film and TV scene.

A Steady Job

In 2007, Jen landed a job on *The Bill Engvall Show*, a TBS sitcom starring comedian Bill Engvall. Jen played his rebellious teenage daughter. The show wasn't getting glowing reviews. Still, it was steady work.

Jen gets a hug from comedian Bill Engvall at a Los Angeles party.

Jen also started getting parts in indie movies. She was drawn to gritty, heavy-duty characters. In 2008, she showed her acting chops with starring roles in *The Poker House* and *The Burning Plain*.

In 2009, *The Bill Engvall Show* was canceled. But Jen didn't need that job anymore. By nineteen, Jen was living alone in L.A., paying her own rent. She was making it in the movies.

> **INDIE MOVIE =**
> a movie that is not made by a big-time Hollywood studio. Indie is short for independent.

Jen played the part of Agnes in *The Poker House*.

The Role She Had to Have

That year, Jen fell in love…with a movie. She became "obsessed" with the script for *Winter's Bone*. The story takes place in rural Missouri. It centers on Ree, a tough-as-nails teenager. She's forced to go face-to-face with the bosses of a dangerous drug ring.

Jen loved how Ree did not see failure as an option. And Jen couldn't either, if she wanted the part. She'd done two auditions in L.A. But the producers were still on the fence. Was Jen too pretty to play rough-and-tumble Ree?

Jen had to prove she had what they wanted. As she tells it, she chased the producers to New York City "like a psycho." She flew on an overnight flight. She had a runny nose. She hadn't washed her hair in a week. She walked into the audition with a "hire-me-or-die" look.

Something clicked. Was it Jen's rough look, her determination, or that final read? Who knows and who cares? Jen got the part!

PRODUCER =
a businessperson who funds a movie project and then makes sure the movie is successful

Jen worked hard for the role of Ree Dolly in *Winter's Bone*.

For *Winter's Bone*, Jen had to learn how to skin a squirrel. Luckily, she had some help. One of her brother's friends brought over a squirrel he'd shot. They skinned it together in her backyard. Jen was so grossed out, she screamed when it was over.

Branching Out

Reviewers were gaga about Jen in *Winter's Bone*. By now, though, Jen had done a lot of serious stuff. It was time to show another side. She signed on to play Mystique in *X-Men: First Class*. A blue mutant was the perfect change of pace!

Jen started filming *X-Men* in London in the fall of 2010. For some reason, though, she couldn't concentrate.

BLUE AND NAKED

Jen (RIGHT) was naked when she played Mystique—that is, unless you count a coat of blue paint as clothes. It took seven makeup artists eight hours to paint on Jen's costume!

She kept messing up her lines. Soon the cause of the problem reared its adorable head. It was Jen's costar, British actor Nicholas Hoult. Jen had a major crush on the guy who played Beast.

Jen holds hands with Nicholas Hoult at an event in May 2012.

By January 2011, Jen and Nicholas were official. Jen later dished that falling for Nicholas was "like a moth flying toward light." She loved how sweet he was. It was that simple. As of fall 2012, they were still as head over heels as ever.

Later that January, Jen got some big news. She had been nominated for an Oscar! She was up for Best Actress for *Winter's Bone.* When she found out, she put her hand over her mouth and gasped.

Not many people had seen Jen in *Winter's Bone*. But nobody forgot Jen on Oscar night that February. Jen didn't expect to win, and she didn't. But she made a splash in her beautiful, sleek red dress. Everybody wanted to know: Who *was* this gorgeous up-and-coming actor anyway?

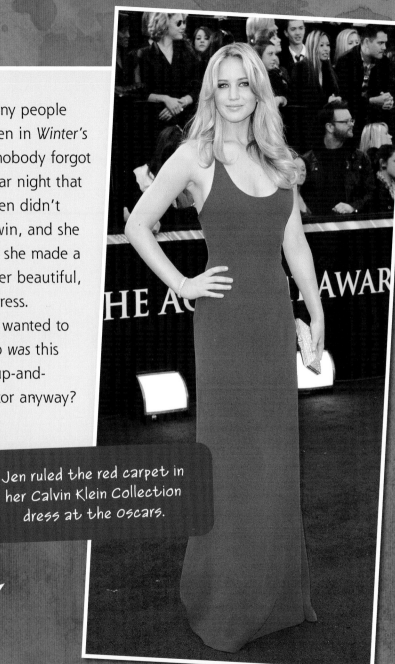

Jen ruled the red carpet in her Calvin Klein Collection dress at the Oscars.

Jen played fierce Katniss Everdeen in the film *The Hunger Games*.

CHAPTER THREE

BECOMING KATNISS

Jen dyed her hair brown for her Katniss role in 2011.

Oscar season was a frenzy of publicity ops. Jen felt like a rag doll. She was squeezed into dresses and pinchy shoes. She was slathered with makeup. She felt a lot like—well, like Katniss getting prepped for the Hunger Games.

PUBLICITY OP =
an event, such as an interview or an autograph signing, that is meant to attract attention or gain support for something

During this time, Jennifer met *The Hunger Games* director Gary Ross. He was starting to do casting for the movie. He and Jen shared a laugh about how she was having her own Katniss experience. She told him what a huge fan she was of the books. (She'd read all three in just four days.) She also asked Ross a personal favor. She asked him not to turn Katniss into a typical, butt-kicking action movie star.

Jen with director Gary Ross in 2012

Ross couldn't have agreed more. In fact, he had been thinking of asking Jen to try out for Katniss for exactly that reason. In *Winter's Bone,* she'd shown that magical combo he was looking for. She showed strength *and* sensitivity.

Ross invited Jen to audition. Needless to say, she took him up on the offer! When the day of her audition came, Jen totally killed. She read the scene when Katniss says good-bye to her little sister, Prim, right before heading off for the Games. Jen was so good, she made the casting director cry.

No Regrets

Soon, Jen got the big offer. It was a dream come true, but Jen had mixed feelings. She knew that this role would make her a huge star—and that terrified her. For three days, Jennifer went back and forth in her mind. In the end, she decided the role was too amazing to pass up. "If I had said no, I would regret it every day," she told *Entertainment Weekly.*

HER SECRET TRICK

Jennifer seems so confident. Yet she often says how scared she is of stuff. Weirdly, Jennifer says that her fears are the secret to her confidence. She has to pretend really hard that she's together. Somewhere along the way, her fake confidence turns real.

Jen takes aim in a scene from *The Hunger Games.*

Best Summer Camp Ever!

In June, Jen headed to the woods of North Carolina to begin training to play Katniss. The schedule was intense. And it was so hot! Jen did track work, stunt drills, and yoga. She also had to learn to shoot a bow and arrow. For that, Jen worked with a former Olympic champ from eastern Europe.

In July, filming began. Jennifer is always nervous starting a movie. "It's like the first day of school," she says. "Is anybody going to like me? Am I going to have any friends? Am I going to disappoint everybody the first day?"

GO, JEN!

Jen shot one hundred arrows a day for three weeks straight. By the end, she was getting four or five bull's-eyes about every ten times. "If somebody holds still, I could kill them," she joked to Jimmy Fallon.

Jen shares a laugh with her *Hunger Games* costars Josh Hutcherson (CENTER) and Liam Hemsworth (RIGHT).

As usual, Jen had nothing to worry about. Filming *The Hunger Games* was a blast. It was like summer camp. She grew super tight with her costars Josh Hutcherson (Peeta) and Liam Hemsworth (Gale).

There were pranks, lots of laughs, and way too many gummy bears. Jen wowed her costars in at least three major ways. One, she was just so incredible as Katniss (and not at all a diva about it). Two, she was always cracking everybody up. Three, she cussed like a dirty comedian.

THE SWEAR JAR

There was a swear jar on set. People had to put in money each time they said a bad word. Gary Ross guesses that Jen put in at least half the money in the jar. Her excuse? "I'm just really immature," she told *People* magazine.

What's Next?

Jen loves acting, but she needs to mix it up. In September 2012, she starred in her first horror movie, *House at the End of the Street*. The next month, she starred in the comedy-drama *Silver Linings Playbook*.

What's next for Jen? Katniss fans are counting down the days until *Catching Fire* comes out in November 2013. Then *Mockingjay* will be split into two movies, to be released in 2014 and 2015.

Where does Jen see herself in ten years? Directing, she hopes, but who knows? "Ten years ago I would have never imagined that I'd be here," she told *Flare* magazine. "So in ten years from now, I might be running a rodeo." If that happens, Jen's fans will be right behind her, screaming "Yee-haw!" all the way!

Jen plays Elissa in the horror film *House at the End of the Street*.

JENNIFER
PICS!

THE WORLD WILL BE WATCHING

THE HUNGER GAM

PEOPLE
CHOICE
AWARD

Liam (LEFT), Jen, and Josh (RIGHT) pose during *The Hunger Games* mall tour in 2012.

SOURCE NOTES

5   *Jennifer Lawrence on Letterman Full Interview HD.* YouTube video, 11:36, posted by The
    SonicSkier, March 22, 2012, http://www.youtube.com/watch?feature=endscreen&v=Rk8
    mO5TNqLE&NR=1 (July 27, 2012).

6   Ibid.

7   Ibid.

7   Ibid.

7   Ibid.

9   *Jennifer Lawrence on David Letterman* [May 2011]. YouTube video, 6:48, posted by
    londondonner, November 13, 2011, http://www.youtube.com/watch?v=KxCPXqj1uBU
    (July 27, 2012).

10 Patty Adams Martinez, "Jennifer Lawrence: If You Think Katniss Has Killer Confidence,
    You Should Meet the Girl Who Plays Her," *Seventeen,* April 2012, 114.

12 Willa Paskin, "The Hunger Games Are Here," *Glamour,* April 2012, 220.

17 Amanda Luttrell Garrigus, "Girl on Fire," *Flare,* June 2011, 126–130.

17 Karen Valby, "The Chosen One," *Entertainment Weekly,* May 27, 2011, 34–43.

17 Martinez, "Jennifer Lawrence," 114.

18 Jerry Rice, "Jennifer Lawrence: Cross-Country Fatigue Helped Give 'Bone' Its Leading
    Lady," *Daily Variety,* December 6, 2010, A4.

18 Stephen Schaefer, "Jennifer Lawrence," *Daily Variety,* October 25, 2010, A5.

20 *Jennifer Lawrence X-Men: First Class Interview.* YouTube video, 1:34, posted by alloy, May
    31, 2011, http://www.youtube.com/watch?v=CrpINI7ft5U (July 27, 2012).

24 Karen Valby, "The Chosen One," *Entertainment Weekly,* May 27, 2011, 34–43.

25 Martinez, "Jennifer Lawrence," 114.

25 *Jennifer Lawrence (3/21/12). Late Night with Jimmy Fallon* video, 4:17, March 21, 2012,
    http://www.latenightwithjimmyfallon.com/video/jennifer-lawrence-3-21-12/1392049
    (July 27, 2012).

26 "Katniss Everdeen," *People,* March 28, 2012, 30–36.

27 Garrigus, "Girl on Fire," 126–130.

MORE JENNIFER INFO

IMDb: Jennifer Lawrence
http://www.imdb.com/name/nm2225369
Jennifer's Internet Movie Database page is packed with photos, quotes, and trivia. It also has the most complete and up-to-date list of everything she's done.

Just Jared Jr.: Jennifer Lawrence
http://www.justjaredjr.com/?s=jennifer+lawrence
This celeb site goes for sweet, not snarky. It shows what Jen is up to from day to day. See her hanging with friends, on her cell, and rockin' adorable footwear. Negative comments will be nixed.

Krohn, Katherine. *Jennifer Lawrence: Star of the Hunger Games.* Minneapolis: Lerner Publications Company, 2012.
Go deeper into Jen's fascinating life with this longer bio.

The Official Website for Jennifer Lawrence
http://jenniferslawrence.com
Obviously, Jen has better things to do than update her site. Go to YouTube for better videos and IMDb for more facts. Still, this site gives key info on how to contact Jen and maybe even get an autograph.

INDEX

PHOTO ACKNOWLEDGMENTS

The images in this book are used with the permission of: © Terry Rice/Getty Images, pp. 2, 29 (top left); © Fred Hayes/Getty Images, pp. 3 (top), 8 (bottom); © Donna Ward/Getty Images, pp. 3 (bottom), 22 (bottom right); © Ray Tamarra/Getty Images, p. 4 (top left); © Brent Perniac/AdMedia/ImageCollect, p. 4 (top right); © Jordan Strauss/WireImage/Getty Images, pp. 4 (bottom), 15; © Jeffrey Ufberg/WireImage/Getty Images, p. 5; AP Photo/Charles Sykes, p. 6; David Fisher/Rex USA, pp. 7, 29 (right); © Alexandra Wyman/Getty Images, p. 8 (top); © Splash News/CORBIS, p. 10; Seth Poppel Yearbook Library, pp. 11, 12; © Daniele Venturelli/WireImage/Getty Images, p. 14 (top left); © Eric Charbonneau/WireImage/Getty Images, pp. 14 (right), 23; Danny Feld/© TBS/Courtesy Everett Collection, p. 14 (bottom left); © Phase 4 Films/Courtesy Everett Collection, p. 16; © Larry Busacca/Getty Images, p. 17; © Roadside Attractions/Courtesy Everett Collection, p. 18; 20th Century Fox/Marvel/The Kobal Collection/Art Resource, NY, p. 19; © Dave M. Bennett/Getty Images, p. 20; © Kevork Djansezian/Getty Images, p. 21; Murray Close/© Lionsgate/Courtesy Everett Collection, pp. 22 (top and bottom left), 25; © Jesse Grant/Getty Images, pp. 26, 29 (bottom left); © Rogue Pictures/Courtesy Everett Collection, p. 27; AP Photo/Chris Pizzello/Invision, p. 28 (top left); © Jason Merritt/Getty Images, p. 28 (right); © Gustavo Caballero/Getty Images, p. 28 (bottom left); © Target Presse Agentur Gmbh/WireImage/Getty Images, p. 29 (top center).

Front cover: © Terry Rice/Getty Images (left); © Jason Merritt/Getty Images (right).
Back cover: © Target Presse Agentur Gmbh/WireImage/Getty Images.

Main body text set in Shannon Std Book 12/18.
Typeface provided by Monotype Typography.